OVERVIEW

Overview

Being decisive can save you time, reduce stress, and reflect positively on you. Decisiveness depends on the existence of three well-honed characteristics – being realistic, self- confident, and action oriented.

A four-step process can be used to help make good decisions. The process involves defining the objective, developing alternative solutions, assessing these options, and choosing the best option.

Decisive people are realistic. You can embody realism by balancing optimism and pessimism, being analytical, and being clear headed. To balance pessimism and optimism as you make decisions, think like a pessimist to identify problems and think like an optimist to identify solutions.

To be analytical, think before acting, learn from past experiences, and identify the pros and cons of each choice. To be clear headed, consider the bigger picture, eliminate bias, and define the objective of the decision.

Self-confidence is necessary for decisiveness. With some concentrated effort you can build your confidence in decision making.

First, be honest about when you're at your best, and when you're not. Once you identify the situations in which you perform best, find ways to operate in those situations instead of situations you don't excel in. You can also work to replace negative thoughts with more positive thoughts – they are infinitely more productive.

Second, cultivate thoroughness by listening carefully, avoiding unnecessary assumptions, and considering the consequences of all decisions.

Third, stay calm to avoid making hasty, inappropriate decisions. Build your ability to remain calm by studying past decisions, planning for potential events, and reviewing your own performance.

Decision making is a process, not just an instantaneous choice. First, determine whether you need to make a decision yet. Second, if action is required, avoid procrastination and make a decision. Finally, implement the decision. Monitoring progress and updating the implementation helps make sure the decision's objective is achieved.

Procrastination is a barrier to decisiveness that can be difficult to overcome. Self-discipline is essential if you want to avoid being tempted by procrastination. This involves being able to set aside immediate pleasures in favor of achieving larger goals in the future.

There are three actions you can take to avoid procrastinating about a decision. First, learn to motivate yourself by focusing on either the rewards of your success or the consequences of failing to achieve your objectives.

Decisiveness

Second, recognize and get rid of excuses by asking whether you're looking for reasons to delay something and determining how you can stay on task. Finally, intermittently allow yourself to procrastinate after forcing yourself to stay on task for a short period of time.

Fear can manifest itself in two ways when it comes to making decisions. First, it can lead you to obsess about decisions. To overcome this way of thinking, you can follow three steps: distract yourself, try to exercise, and write down some steps you'll take to help you reach a decision.

Fear can also make you afraid to make the wrong decision. But it's important to realize that a lot of things are beyond your control. To escape this fear, focus your attention on what you can do and away from the outcome of the decision. This involves reframing your thoughts in terms of the actions you can take.

Information overload is when you have so much information that it prevents you from making a particular decision. Signs of information overload include confusion, inability to relax, and difficulty sleeping.

To overcome information overload when it comes to making decisions, you can follow four steps. First, list the reasons that you're taking too long to make your decision. Second, for each reason, write a sentence to contradict it. Third, set a deadline to make your decision. And fourth, budget your time so that you can accomplish your decision-making tasks within your deadline.

CHAPTER ONE

Developing Character for Decisiveness

Being decisive

Perhaps you struggle with decisions or would like to improve your ability to make decisions. Maybe you respect the decisiveness of some of your colleagues and wish you could be like them. Do you wonder how they're able to make the right decisions quickly and confidently?

Decision making can sometimes be very challenging. It can be hard to make decisions when you're dealing with uncertainty, complexity, and risk. Unfamiliarity and fear of consequences, known and unknown, can also make decision making difficult.

The way individuals handle decisions can mean the difference between decisiveness and procrastination. What's the difference? Typically, decisive individuals tend to possess three key character traits: realism, self-confidence, and an orientation to action. The ability to balance optimism and pessimism helps them be realistic. Self-confidence allows decisive people to make decisions with conviction. Being action oriented helps them avoid procrastinating.

Individuals who are decisive enjoy some significant advantages over their less decisive counterparts. They're able to save time, are less stressed, and are regarded positively by others.

See each benefit, in order, for an example of it in action.

Able to save time

Stacy, an advertising executive, is asked to make an important decision quickly – whether to renew traditional commercial ads or invest in social media. The stakes are high because a false move will undoubtedly result in lost market share. She quickly comes back with a decision that is both comprehensive and viable.

Less stressed

A coworker asks how she made the decision while seemingly remaining so calm. Stacy tells her she manages her stress by getting straight to work on making the decision. She explains that this helps her feel more productive and maintain a sense of control when otherwise she could easily become overwhelmed.

Regarded positively

The coworker is genuinely impressed with Stacy's decision-making ability. The rest of the stakeholders are also impressed. They're so confident in Stacy that they give her full support to pursue a social media campaign.

Question

What are some of the benefits of being decisive?

Options:

1. You'll save time
2. You'll be less stressed

Decisiveness

3. You'll be regarded positively
4. You'll need fewer resources
5. You'll avoid poor choices

Answer:

Option 1: This option is correct. Decisive people make a decision and get right to work implementing the decision. They avoid wasting time by not procrastinating.

Option 2: This option is correct. You'll be less stressed because, having made your decision promptly, you can get to work on implementing it.

Option 3: This option is correct. Decisiveness is a trait highly regarded by others and will reflect positively on you.

Option 4: This option is incorrect. Being decisive won't necessarily reduce the resources you need.

Option 5: This option is incorrect. Being decisive doesn't guarantee that all your choices will be good ones. However, using an organized method to make decisions should improve their quality.

Defining objectives

One additional characteristic decisive people tend to share is that they're quite systematic. They typically have some kind of process they follow to make decisions easier. You, too, can use an effective four-step process to help you be decisive. The steps are to define the objective, create options, assess options, and choose the best option.

The first step to take when making a decision is to define the objective of the decision. Ask yourself what it is you want to achieve. This will help you focus your efforts.

At this point, you need to be clear about the issue you're making the decision about. The more you know and understand the issue, the more likely you'll be to make an appropriate decision.

You can ask questions to determine if you're focusing on the right issue. An effective way to do this is to ask "Why?" until you reach the point where asking "Why?" doesn't break the issue or problem down any further.

Decisiveness

Recent problems indicate that a company's database needs attention. John, the engineer, doesn't know the extent of the problem – does the system need to be repaired, updated, or replaced?

John sits down with the incident reports to investigate the problem. He jots down some questions he'll need to answer in order to understand what's at the root of the problem.

After analyzing the information and talking to coworkers with knowledge of the incidences, John determines the database needs more capacity. With a clear objective in mind, he's confident he's addressing the right issue when he sets out to make a decision about how to increase capacity.

Creating options

Now that you understand the issue clearly, you can move on to step two – create options. Exploring the issue to develop viable alternatives will help you make the best decision.

Consult with others to broaden your perspective on an issue and become aware of alternatives. You may even find that you're able to combine some of the options.

Recall John, the database engineer who needs to increase the capacity of his organization's database. Well, after speaking with functional department heads, John has developed alternatives.

He can replace the system entirely or upgrade it.

And if it needs to be upgraded, John has to decide between contracting the work out or doing it in-house.

Question

Creating options means developing potential choices that are viable ways to achieve the decision's objective.

Is this statement true or false?

Options:
1. True 2. False

Answer:
Creating options is the second step in the decision-making process. Striving to create unbiased and reasonable options will improve your decisions.

Assessing options

Once you're confident you've identified realistic options, you can move on to the third step – assess options. Compare the options to the objective you defined in step one by determining the risk, implications, and feasibility of each option.

See each criterion for assessing the options you've identified for more information.

Risk

Uncertainty leads to risk. Analyze the risk associated with each option to determine which option has the least risk, or perhaps more important, the most manageable risk. Sometimes the deciding factor in risk is the cost to manage it – be sure to determine this too.

Implications

After analyzing the risks, evaluate the potential implications of each option from various perspectives. This can help you uncover unexpected consequences. You should also weigh the pros and cons of each choice.

Feasibility

Once you've evaluated the implications, determine the financial feasibility of each option. Assessing feasibility helps you understand which option provides the most benefit for the least cost.

Recall John, the database engineer with the objective to increase capacity of the database. He's created options, and now he needs to assess those options.

The system's capacity can be increased by upgrading it. And the risk and consequences associated with upgrading are more acceptable than replacing the system.

Having a contractor do the work isn't any more risky than doing the work in-house, but working in-house does have its benefits. This option is less expensive. But even better, it keeps the expertise and knowledge of the system in-house.

Choosing the best option

Now that you've assessed each option, it's time to choose the best one. Several actions can help you perform the final evaluation. To begin, revisit the objective to make sure it's fresh and clear in your mind.

Next, remain objective – be vigilant in making sure your personal biases don't influence your thinking.

Finally, assign priority to key factors so you know which ones are most important to making a successful decision.

Once you've thoroughly reviewed the options, choose the one that best meets the objective of the decision. Look for the option that offers the best combination of manageable risk, implications, and financial feasibility.

John, the database engineer, is now ready to choose the best option. As he sets to work he revisits the objective – to increase capacity. Then he reviews the options, being careful to question his thinking. He doesn't want bias to impact his decision.

Finally, he decides on the best option – to buy the necessary hardware and do the work in-house. The risk is manageable, the implications of keeping the knowledge in-house are beneficial, and the option is financially feasible.

Question

Ted's team has been less productive lately and he needs to decide how to remedy this.

Sequence the steps Ted might take to make this decision.

Options:

A. Ted determines that the real issue is poor communication

B. Ted considers team and individual communication coaching sessions to help improve communication

C. Ted knows individual coaching would address specific issues with team members but a team approach would build relationships as it addresses individual issues

D. Ted realizes he prefers group sessions, so he works to keep that prejudice out of his evaluation of which option is best

Answer:

Ted determines that the real issue is poor communication is ranked the first step in the process.

Defining the objective of the decision is the first step Ted needs to take. This will guide his decision.

Ted considers team and individual communication coaching sessions to help improve communication is ranked the second step in the process.

In the second step, Ted needs to create viable options. The better his options, the better his final decision will be.

Ted knows individual coaching would address specific issues with team members but a team approach would build relationships as it addresses individual issues is ranked the third step in the process.

Assessing options, the third step, is essential to understanding how well each meets the objective of the decision. Ted will have to decide which option will best improve communication.

Ted realizes he prefers group sessions, so he works to keep that prejudice out of his evaluation of which option is best is ranked the fourth step in the process.

Step four, choosing the best option, requires objectivity and determining which option is most likely to be successful. Ted has realized a personal bias, which he then works to keep out of his decision.

Balancing optimism and pessimism

Decisive individuals tend to be realistic, self-confident, and action oriented. Being realistic is a key characteristic when it comes to assessing alternatives and choosing the most appropriate one to achieve your objective. Being realistic actually involves at least three traits: being able to balance optimism and pessimism, being analytical, and being clear headed.

Being decisive doesn't just mean making as many decisions as possible – it means making good decisions quickly and confidently.

If your thinking is too negative or too positive, that will impair your decision-making abilities.

One trait that makes decisive individuals more realistic than indecisive people is their ability to balance optimism and pessimism in their thinking.

Optimism is a way of thinking defined by the general view that life and outcomes will be positive. You can use optimism to explore possibilities and generate solutions.

Optimists believe goals can be achieved in the long run. Believing that failure is a temporary setback on the road to success tends to make optimism more productive and motivating than pessimism.

However, extreme optimism can lead you to overlook, ignore, or miss problems.

By contrast, pessimism is a way of thinking defined by the general view that life and outcomes will be negative.

Although pessimism creates a generally negative view, thinking pessimistically occasionally is actually a good way to identify problems and overcome obstacles.

At its extreme, pessimism is very demotivating because a negative outcome is assumed to be inevitable.

Consider this example. Suppose you're planning an outdoor event to demonstrate innovative search and rescue equipment. Your way of thinking – whether overly optimistic, overly pessimistic, or balanced – will influence your decision about how to demonstrate the equipment.

See each approach to learn how it might influence your decision in this example.

Overly optimistic

Instead of planning an alternative indoor option, you choose to believe the weather will be agreeable on the day of the event. This decision is risky and may lead to failure.

Overly pessimistic

Alternatively, if you're overly pessimistic, the event may never get planned. Or the idea of planning an outdoor event may be immediately understood as too risky because you know the weather will be bad. If an outdoor event will be more effective, immediately dismissing this as an option limits the potential for a positive outcome.

Balance

Decisiveness

Now suppose you pursue balance. Optimistically, you acknowledge that bad weather might actually be beneficial because rescues often occur in inclement weather. Pessimistically, you identify the problem of your guests being subjected to the bad weather. Combining the two approaches, you might decide to build an outdoor observation area to protect your guests. Or you may plan an indoor alternative venue to simulate the true outdoor use of the equipment. Either way, you're prepared and a positive outcome is more likely.

When you consider a situation from both angles and apply a balanced approach, you identify the potential for both good and bad outcomes of a decision. This prepares you to achieve your goal in a realistic way.

Question

Maria needs to make a decision about whether to train her employees on a new sales procedure. She knows she doesn't have the money to hire a trainer to deliver the necessary instruction to all affected employees.

Which example demonstrates Maria being realistic while making her decision about whether to train her employees?

Options:

1. Maria decides it's not possible to go ahead with the training because she can't afford it

2. Maria decides to hire a trainer because the eventual increase in sales will balance out the cost of the training

3. Maria decides to get her managers trained and then have them train their employees

Answer:

Option 1: This option is incorrect. Maria is being overly pessimistic. By forgoing the training, Maria's also limiting the potential for increased sales.

Option 2: This option is incorrect. Maria's optimism about the new sales procedure is unrealistic. She's failed to solve the problem of not having the money to provide the training.

Option 3: This is the correct option. A balanced approach allows Maria to recognize the problem but also find a way of dealing with it.

Being analytical

Being analytical is the second trait that helps individuals be decisive. Analytical thinkers study relevant information to understand consequences and develop options. Specifically, being analytical when making decisions means thinking before acting, learning from the past, and identifying the pros and cons of each option.

When making a decision, think before acting. To begin, analyze the objective to make sure you understand it. Then identify options that will help you achieve the objective. These are your potential decisions. Finally, consider the consequences of each option – like who might be affected. You may also need to gather input from others to help you properly analyze, understand, and identify options. Decisive people tend to make decisions quickly but only after careful analysis.

Suppose Daniel and Stella are supervisors in a call center. They've received a directive from their manager – determine why a new procedure for escalating calls to managers isn't working. The truth is the procedure is fine. There just aren't enough managers to handle the number of calls being escalated.

Daniel reviews the procedure and concludes that it's adequate. Without further consideration, he sends an e-mail to his team members reminding them of the importance of properly following procedure. Daniel has failed to uncover the root of the problem and his decision is ineffective.

Stella analyzes the procedure, but then speaks to members of her team. She learns that the procedure works as it's designed to work, but unfortunately when calls can't be escalated due to high call volume, it's ineffective. Stella makes the best decision given the circumstances – one that will reduce the number of calls being escalated and make sure enough managers are available to handle them.

Perhaps you mentioned how learning from the past can help you to identify what works or to generate new ideas. Both are true. Draw on your own experiences and the experiences of others to learn from the past.

Review decisions critically to avoid taking the wrong lesson from a past experience. Failure or success in the past doesn't necessarily mean the outcome will be the same in your situation.

Instead, consider the variables that influenced the original decision. For instance, consider who made the decision, its timing, and the circumstances surrounding the decision. If you do, you'll have a better understanding of what information from the past is relevant to the decision you're making.

Decisiveness

For example, suppose Aaron is thinking of implementing a system to support interdepartmental collaboration. However, when he studies how the same system was implemented elsewhere, he finds it hasn't worked.

But upon closer review, he discovers that he has access to better equipment. So the earlier failure doesn't rule out the option.

If he had taken the previous implementation at face value, Aaron may not have realized that the solution can work with adequate system capabilities.

Identifying the pros and cons of each option is also an important analysis tool.

Sometimes it's easy to focus on what's positive about an option and simply ignore or overlook what's not so good about it.

For example, a new power source may solve your energy deficiencies but be too expensive to justify financially. Knowing this, you can search for alternatives.

Question

Trey has to make a decision about how to proceed with an investment. Which examples show Trey being analytical as he makes his decision?

Options:

1. Trey asks more experienced brokers for their input
2. Trey researches similar decisions to learn about potential outcomes
3. Trey is impressed with the stability of one option but is not so impressed with its relatively low rate of return
4. Trey recognizes that he doesn't need to reinvent the wheel, and follows the example of a recent, similar decision he studied

5. Trey recognizes the consequences that one decision could cause for clients, but decides to eliminate this option to avoid complicating the decision even further

Answer:

Option 1: This option is correct. Trey is being analytical by drawing on the experience of others.

Option 2: This option is correct. Learning from past experience is a great way to explore decisions.

Option 3: This option is correct. To make a good decision, analyze both the pros and cons of each option.

Option 4: This option is incorrect. Analyze past successful decisions to understand what made them successful – it's not appropriate to simply implement the decision exactly as it was in the past.

Option 5: This option is incorrect. It will make the decision more difficult, but consequences for people can't be ignored.

Being clear headed

The final trait decisive individuals tend to possess is clear headedness. In terms of decision making, clear headedness means seeing the bigger picture, being unbiased, and defining an objective for the decision.

Seeing the bigger picture is about making sure you understand all that's involved with a decision. This can be difficult. For instance, it can be easy to assume you know what to do if you've made a similar decision before. Other times you might be too close to the situation to see it clearly. Or you might be so involved with the details that you lose perspective.

Gain perspective by considering new ideas, studying the ideas of others, and thinking outside the box. Perspective helps you see the big picture and understand what's involved in the decision you're making.

Being unbiased is also essential to being clear headed. If you allow personal biases to influence your thinking, you might make bad decisions.

Bias can cloud your thinking if you're too emotionally attached to a particular outcome. Suppose you've been waiting for your chance to upgrade your company's security system because you've had the perfect solution selected for years. In this circumstance, you may not give other ideas the consideration they deserve when it's time to select a new system.

Objectivity can be particularly difficult to achieve when you have many options to consider, the available options involve a lot of uncertainty, or your decision will have consequences for people.

Being as objective as possible helps ensure bias doesn't influence your decisions. Knowing the facts, considering the context, and timing the decision can help you remain objective. It's also important to know who's accountable for the decision.

See each component to learn how it can help you be objective.

Facts

Know the facts relevant to the decision you're making. Define the level of detail needed to make the decision and stick to it. Considering more detail than necessary is a waste of time and can lead you to make the wrong decision if you're not careful.

Context

Consider the context of the decision. This includes the political, financial, and mass media environments.

Time

Make sure you know how much time you have to achieve the objective of the decision. Timing can impact what can be achieved.

Who's accountable

Decisiveness

Make sure you know who's accountable because you'll need their help to implement the decision. Without their support, you might not be able to achieve your objective.

Defining an objective is an essential part of any decision-making process. Essentially, the objective of any decision is what you want to achieve by making and implementing the decision.

For example, when you decide which clothes to wear every day, you must take your objective into account. If your objective is to dress appropriately for the office, you wouldn't choose to wear your gym clothes. If you're dressing for the park, you wouldn't choose a business suit.

The same logic applies when you make decisions. You need to know what you're trying to achieve; otherwise you're not likely to achieve it.

Work to define your objective by asking questions until you clearly understand the issue or problem underlying the decision. Achieving clarity about the issues will help you make the right decision.

For example, suppose Camille, an executive, has been asked to purchase new presentation equipment for her company. Camille begins by speaking to all the functional managers to find out what features are important to them.

Based on experience, she suspects she'll only gain the board's support if she picks the most inexpensive option. However, she goes ahead with collecting details – including price – about various systems.

Then Camille defines the objective. Her decision needs to satisfy the needs of the functional managers and offer the best price.

Question

Ursula needs to decide which community events to sponsor. Ursula has been making this decision for her company for years, so she doesn't expect it to be too difficult.

In which examples is Ursula being clear headed?

Options:

1. Ursula decides to support her favorites, just like she does every year

2. Ursula considers which option will be best suited to the current political environment

3. Ursula checks to make sure she knows what it is she needs to accomplish through sponsorship

4. Ursula is so familiar with making this decision she makes assumptions about who will be helping her implement it

Answer:

Option 1: This option is incorrect. Letting personal bias guide decisions isn't appropriate.

Option 2: This option is correct. It's important to consider the political environment when making a decision. What could be a viable option under some circumstances may not be a viable option under other circumstances.

Option 3: This option is correct. Focusing on what the objective of the decision is supposed to be is essential to making a good decision.

Option 4: This option is incorrect. Knowing who's responsible for helping to implement a decision is critical because without their support, you may not be able to properly implement it.

Be self-confident

In addition to being realistic and action oriented, decisive people tend to have self-confidence. High self-esteem gives them a positive view of themselves, and their sense of self-efficacy gives them a belief that
they can achieve what they set out to achieve.

Lack of confidence stems largely from negative thoughts about yourself – for example your appearance, your intelligence, your creativity, your social skills, or your educational or social background. A lack of self-confidence can damage your decision-making abilities. Low self-confidence may lead to inaction, self-limitation, avoiding responsibility, and doubting your decisions.

See each consequence of low self-confidence to learn more about it.

Inaction

Lack of confidence in your ability may lead to inaction. You may prefer to do nothing because you're afraid of making the wrong decision. However, this is likely to make you feel defeated.

For example, afraid of making the wrong decision, Helena waits for better information and seeks more and more input from professionals. Meanwhile, she's growing increasingly worried about the decision she needs to make.

Self-limitation

People who suffer from low self-confidence tend to place unnecessary limitations on their capabilities. Instead of challenging themselves and taking calculated risks, they play it safe and stay within their comfort zone. This can also set limitations on the decisions they make.

For instance, instead of investigating his options, Jim renews his contract with his current Internet supplier. While this might be the best decision, Jim can't know for sure because he didn't investigate his options.

Avoiding responsibility

Avoiding responsibility can be another side-effect of low self-confidence. Individuals who suffer from a lack of confidence tend to defer responsibility for making decisions because they believe others can make better decisions.

For example, when Jane is asked to take charge of a project decision, she says she'll do the necessary work but isn't comfortable making any decisions.

Doubting your decisions

Even after they've made a decision, people with low self-confidence may remain troubled. If they don't trust the decision they've made, they're likely to be fearful, anxious, or worried about whether they made the right decision.

Decisiveness

Larry, for instance, has just decided on the best course of action for a business venture. As he gets ready to distribute the details of his decision, he is plagued by doubts about whether he's doing the right thing. Needless to say, this doesn't inspire confidence from others.

Self-confidence is important to decision making because it generates a sense that things are under control and being handled properly. Self-confident people tend to challenge themselves more, which helps them achieve more. They also tend to set higher expectations, which removes limitations and can promote greater success. Self-confident people also tend to handle change with more ease. This helps them avoid procrastination and helps build trust in their decision-making ability.

Question

Why is self-confidence an advantage when it comes to decision making?

Options:

1. You'll make decisions faster
2. You'll demand more of yourself
3. You'll have trust in the decisions you make
4. You'll be more willing to take responsibility for your actions
5. You'll instinctively know which direction to take
6. You'll feel more comfortable sharing accountability

Answer:

Option 1: This option is correct. Self-confidence removes many obstacles to inaction, such as fear and overanalysis, and allows you to make decisions more efficiently.

Option 2: This option is correct. Believing in your abilities will help you overcome any self-imposed limitations. You'll also be more likely to challenge yourself to achieve more.

Option 3: This option is correct. Self-confidence helps free you from crippling self-doubt about the quality of your decisions.

Option 4: This option is correct. Having self-confidence means you're more willing to take on the burden of making decisions rather than leaving it to others. This in turn means taking more responsibility for your actions.

Option 5: This option is incorrect. You'll have increased confidence in your ability to make decisions, but you'll still need to carefully analyze your options before choosing the right one.

Option 6: This option is incorrect. Building self-confidence will help you take accountability for your decisions.

Be honest

Increasing your self-confidence can help you make decisions with confidence. There are three things you can do to build your decision-making confidence: be honest about when you're at your best and when you're not, be thorough, and be calm.

Begin to build self-confidence for decision making by being honest about when you're at your best and when you're not. You may be able to rely on intuition to tell you where your strengths lie. But analysis can certainly help. Start by recalling instances of success or when you've felt you've done well in the past.

Perhaps you noted that you were at your best when you were prepared or were collaborating in small groups.

Alternatively, perhaps you determined you were not at your best when you were unsure of the value of what you were doing, you had too many deadlines at once, or you were required to speak in front of a large audience.

Once you identify the circumstances that play to your strengths and those that do not, you can improve your confidence by acting on that knowledge. Simply increase as much as possible the number of times you're in situations when you're at your best, and decrease the number of times you're in situations when you're not at your best.

You can also work to remove limiting thoughts from your way of thinking. Limiting thoughts are negative thoughts, and they stand in your way of being successful and confident.

If you find yourself always saying "I never have enough time," say to yourself instead "I will have enough time to do what I need to do."

As you replace negative thoughts with positive ones, you'll find yourself having more self-confidence. You can use this approach with any negative self-talk.

Be careful that you don't turn self-confidence into over-confidence. Having too much self-confidence can lead to arrogance.

Arrogance can be an obstacle to success. It can lead to rash judgments simply because you "know" you're right. This can't possibly be true all the time.

Also, many people find it difficult to work with arrogant coworkers. Arrogant individuals tend to leave coworkers feeling underappreciated and even disrespected. Under these circumstances, coworkers may not trust the decisions made by their arrogant colleagues.

Question

Which statements demonstrate being honest when making decisions?

Options:

Decisiveness

1. Replace negative thoughts about yourself with positive thoughts
2. Try to be in situations where you know you'll be at your best more often
3. Avoid unnecessarily exposing yourself to situations where you know you won't be at your best
4. Always refuse to work in situations where you know you won't be at your best
5. Listen to the voice in your head when it says you're not capable – it's usually right

Answer:

Option 1: This option is correct. Negative thoughts limit success. Replace negative thoughts with positive ones and you should see an increase in your confidence.

Option 2: This option is correct. Having made an honest assessment of your strengths, you need to seek out situations where you know you'll be at your best.

Option 3: This option is correct. Focus on minimizing your involvement in situations where you won't be at your best.

Option 4: This option is incorrect. You may need to work in situations where you won't be at your best. Do what you can to improve your capabilities in these situations.

Option 5: This option is incorrect. Listening to negative messages of self-doubt negatively impacts confidence and decision-making abilities.

Be thorough

Being thorough is another way to build your confidence in your decision-making abilities. Paying careful attention to detail when making decisions helps you know you've covered what you need to be successful. This will naturally help you become more confident about the decisions you make. As you make decisions, listen carefully, don't make assumptions, and consider consequences – this will help you be thorough.

First, listen carefully. Good listeners tend to be better problem solvers – something that can come in handy when making decisions. So it can be beneficial to improve your listening skills. There are several ways to do this:
- take notes to help you focus, show interest, and provide a valuable resource later,
- hold your judgment until after you've heard everything – otherwise you may misjudge the information,

Decisiveness

- ask questions to clarify your understanding or increase your knowledge,
- concentrate on facts and figures to avoid emotional reactions to the information that can lead you to think with bias,
- be aware of your personal biases and keep them out of your decision-making process, and
- check your enthusiasm to make sure you haven't become caught up in hype – instead listen to all the information before giving your support to any idea.

George needs to make a decision about which material to use in a new interior wall paint. He's asked Kareem, a chemical engineer, to talk with him about his potential choices. As Kareem speaks, George starts to doodle cartoon characters on a piece of paper.

George is very skeptical about what Kareem is telling him. Past experience tells him Kareem's idea is unlikely to work. However, George hears him out and learns that advances in engineering allow the material to be used effectively now. When Kareem finishes, George asks questions to get clarification on things he didn't understand. This helps him open his mind to the possibilities.

George finds himself getting rather excited about the idea. He is surprised because he had been so skeptical. Now he's so convinced that he takes Kareem's information at face value. George is pleased that his decision is clear – he'll use the material Kareem has suggested.

Question

Which elements of listening carefully did George use properly?

Options:

1. Take notes
2. Hold judgment
3. Concentrate on facts and figures
4. Be aware of your personal biases
5. Check your enthusiasm

Answer:

Option 1: This option is incorrect. George didn't take notes about what Kareem was saying. In fact, he drew cartoon characters.

Option 2: This option is correct. Past experience makes George question Kareem's advice, but he hears him out before judging the information.

Option 3: This option is incorrect. Considering facts and figures is a great way to remain objective. George should have asked Kareem to support his advice with empirical evidence.

Option 4: This option is correct. George was skeptical, but instead of allowing past experience to result in personal bias, he listened to what Kareem had to say before judging the information.

Option 5: This option is incorrect. George was excited by what he was hearing. Instead of checking his enthusiasm, he got caught up in what he chose to believe.

If you want to be thorough when making decisions, don't make assumptions. Typically, assumptions tend to support preferences – which don't always lead to the most appropriate decisions.

Instead, focus on facts when making decisions. This will help you remain objective and draw conclusions that are

Decisiveness

right for the goal of the decision, not your personal preferences.

Assumptions can be dangerous because they're rarely based on fact. You can begin to remove their influence on your decision making by avoiding some common assumptions: promoting stereotypes, perceiving "different" as "negative," thinking one approach is sufficient, and making assumptions about people.

However, while avoiding assumptions is typically best, sometimes you need to make assumptions to make decisions. When you're planning or executing decisions, you can't know everything. For example, you can't know if frost will ruin crops, but you may have to assume it will in order to make important decisions about how to manage your crops.

Making assumptions can be useful in decision making. Assumptions can allow you to draw reasoned conclusions that are based on logic or intuition and to move forward when you have no facts to guide you.

If you have to base a decision on assumption, check regularly to make sure it's still appropriate. If not, update the plan or implementation of the decision based on the new information.

Finally, thoroughness requires you to consider the consequences of decisions. For example, suppose you have a choice between upgrading a facility and building a new one – you need to properly identify the consequences of each decision.

Next, determine how to manage the consequences you've identified. If one consequence of upgrading is reduced capacity during the upgrade, you need to decide how you're going to handle this, for instance.

Also, make sure your proposed responses to the consequences are viable. Otherwise you'll fail to manage the consequences to the detriment of the decision. Suppose, for example, you decided to run around-the-clock shifts during the plant upgrade. But this turns out to be impossible because some machinery will have to be taken offline completely. This makes 24-hour shifts a nonviable response.

Question

Which statements reflect being thorough?

Options:

1. Jotting down key information can help to improve your concentration and help you recall key information

2. Relying on what you know to be true from experience can help you draw adequate conclusions

3. Focusing on facts can help you manage the potential downfalls of having to rely on assumptions during planning

4. Using what feels right to you as a guide is a good way to consider the various key factors that go into making a decision

5. Studying the potential outcomes of decisions will help you properly evaluate your alternatives

Answer:

Option 1: This option is correct. Taking notes is a great way to enhance your listening skills because it can help you remain focused.

Option 2: This option is incorrect. It's important to avoid making assumptions. By nature they're risky, so instead be thorough.

Decisiveness

Option 3: This option is correct. If you need to make assumptions, use facts to determine if planning assumptions need to be updated.

Option 4: This option is incorrect. Be aware of your personal biases – they'll negatively impact your ability to fairly assess information. This can lead to bad decisions.

Option 5: This option is correct. Considering the consequences of each of your alternatives is important to making and implementing the best decision.

Be calm

Another way to build confidence in decision making is to be calm. Decisions may need to be made quickly and without complete information – this can be typical during a crisis. Failure to remain calm can lead to hasty decisions that can have negative impacts. So how can you improve your ability to stay calm during a crisis?

First, draw on the experience of others, especially those who are known for remaining calm, by studying their past decisions. Study both their successful and unsuccessful outcomes to learn the most. Drawing on this experience can guide you when you need to make good decisions in a crisis.

For instance, Connor needs to appoint a project leader and he's nervous. He has no experience making decisions that impact people. Connor studies decisions of other leaders to learn how they've made this type of decision.

You can pick examples of great decision makers from business, politics, or even the military to learn how they dealt with decisions during crisis. This is a risk-free way to gain invaluable insight from real- world events.

Planning can also help. Although you can't plan for a crisis, you can plan to respond to potential events. Having a plan to deal with both problems and opportunities that come up can help you remain calm and make appropriate decisions.

For instance, Jody knows an attractive overseas market could open up for his company's products, so he plans for that possibility. Being prepared to act will be a real advantage to his organization.

Finally, reviewing your own performance can help you recognize where you've done well and where you haven't. Applying what you learn to future decisions will improve your performance during stressful situations.

For example, Heather's having a hard time understanding the value of a decision she's making. She realizes she's getting flustered and rushing to make a decision. She also realizes she won't make the best decision this way.

Once you identify this, you can work to find ways to remain calm. You may want to try exercise or meditation, for instance.

Question

Which statements accurately depict ways to learn to remain calm?

Options:

1. Analyzing other people's decisions can help you learn how to stay calm and make a good decision

2. Preparing for potential events can help you reduce the stress involved with having to make a decision quickly

3. Studying your own decisions as you gain experience to see where you need to improve can help you focus your efforts and remain calm

4. Examining the decisions of others won't help you because they don't have the same context

5. Identifying what could happen during a crisis will help you remain calm in the event it happens

Answer:

Option 1: This option is correct. Studying decisions made by other individuals is a risk-free way to learn how to handle your decisions.

Option 2: This option is correct. Planning for potential events promotes calmness because having a plan builds confidence in your ability to deal with these events.

Option 3: This option is correct. Reviewing your performance to understand your ability to make decisions during a crisis will improve your ability to make good decisions.

Option 4: This option is incorrect. Studying decisions made during crises can help you learn how to remain calm, regardless of context.

Option 5: This option is incorrect. Knowing what could happen isn't enough; you need to prepare a plan of action to follow if it does happen.

Question

Identify examples of how to build self-confidence for decision making.

Options:

1. Cara realizes she's having negative thoughts about her abilities and works hard to think more positively

Decisiveness

2. Charlie allows Rose to finish expressing her ideas about the new bill collection procedure before asking questions

3. Husain realizes he's starting to panic over the potential outcomes, so he prepares for each one

4. Marta avoids making a decision because she knows she's not capable of making a good decision

5. Louise knows from past experience that upgrading the system will be inadequate

Answer:

Option 1: This option is correct. Cara's limiting thoughts can negatively impact confidence. Try to turn negative thoughts into positive ones.

Option 2: This option is correct. Listening without interrupting will help Charlie be more thorough as he makes his decision.

Option 3: This option is correct. Preparing for potential outcomes could help Husain feel more calm about the decision he's making.

Option 4: This option is incorrect. Marta needs to stop listening to her negative thoughts and build her self-confidence by replacing them with positive ones.

Option 5: This option is incorrect. Drawing on past experience can be helpful, but Louise needs to make sure she's not making an invalid assumption.

Decide whether to make a decision

Being realistic and self-confident are two traits of decisive individuals. Together they provide a solid foundation for the third trait – being action oriented. And in fact, the ability to act with assertion improves as self-confidence grows. Action oriented individuals work on tasks that need to be done without making excuses or procrastinating.

A set of three interrelated actions can help you to be action oriented and make decisions. First, decide whether you need to make a decision. Next, if a decision is merited, immediately set out to work on making the decision. Finally, implement the decision.

So the first step is deciding whether you actually need to make a decision. Some problems and opportunities don't require action, and doing nothing in these cases is the best choice.

There are legitimate reasons not to act. For example, you may not be the right person to make the decision. In

Decisiveness

this case, you should bring the matter to whoever has the authority to act.

Another good reason to do nothing is if you have insufficient information to make an appropriate decision. For instance, suppose you've noted an anomaly in production statistics. Reacting immediately, without more data, may be premature. Instead, you might ask that the process be monitored so you can collect more data.

On the other hand, you may have sufficient, appropriate information that indicates no action is required. For instance, perhaps a concern has surfaced about whether a plant meets a safety code. You have recently completed a safety review using new guidelines, so you know it's safe. In this case, no action is required.

Imagine that Yolanda and Harold have the same decision to make. Both individuals have become aware of a dip in sales for the last reporting period. The question they're both asking is "Does anything need to be done about this now?"

Yolanda reviews the information and acknowledges the decrease in sales. However, sales dips are historically common because of seasonal influences. Yolanda decides to carefully monitor sales and not take any corrective action yet.

Harold reviews the sales data. He immediately becomes alarmed about the decrease in sales. He reviews historical data and sees that this is common for the time of year. Unsure about what he should do, he distances himself from the matter by concentrating on his daily tasks.

Question

In the previous example of Yolanda and Harold, who is procrastinating?

Options:
1. Yolanda
2. Harold

Answer:

Option 1: This option is incorrect. Yolanda isn't procrastinating. She reacted properly to this situation. She's reviewed relevant information and realized that the right decision is to do nothing at this time. Because she's planned how she'll monitor the situation, she can feel confident in her decision not to take any action until it's clear there is a problem to be addressed.

Option 2: This is the correct option. Harold is procrastinating. Despite the fact that he has sufficient information, he continues to focus on other tasks instead of making a decision.

Make the decision

If you determine that action is required, immediately set out to work on making the decision. This is the second action. Try not to make excuses, such as arguing that data collection will be tedious, or fret about potential negative consequences. It's important that you act decisively.

The most effective way to avoid procrastination is to immediately start the decision-making process. If you need more incentive, consider some important reasons not to procrastinate.

First, making decisions right away frees you to do other tasks. Procrastinating is a waste of time and abilities. Suppose an opportunity arises that you'd like to take advantage of, but you're already procrastinating an important decision.

Making a decision can launch you into productive action. Often the most difficult thing about making a decision is overcoming the mental barrier to making it.

After you make the decision, you may find the challenge isn't as big as you thought.

The quality of a decision depends on the quality of the decision-making process.

Knowing that you'll have to explain your decision and your progress to others may encourage you to carefully make the best decision.

If you can justify your decision, you may also find it easier to take action.

Becky knows she needs to take action to resolve a problem. Lower than anticipated demand for her company's products means she must make a decision about how to best respond to a lack of work. Her objective is to find a way to keep everyone working. Her approach will be different depending on whether she is procrastinating or not procrastinating.

See either "Procrastinating" or "Not procrastinating" for an example of Becky doing each.

Procrastinating

Becky is in the middle of a task. Instead of putting it aside, she decides to finish it before figuring out how to keep everyone working. Once a spot opens up in her schedule, she starts to worry about the potential negative consequences. And even though she has relevant information, she insists she needs more. As she collects more information she becomes confused and puts the decision on the back burner again.

Not procrastinating

Becky is in the middle of a task, but she determines it's lower priority and sets it aside to tackle the problem. Becky collects information pertinent to the decision and carefully analyzes it to make sure she understands what

Decisiveness

she'll need to do to get everyone working. Once she considers her options, she chooses the best one – taking customized orders until normal work levels are achieved. Next, she plans how she'll implement the decision.

Question

Which examples demonstrate someone being action oriented?

Options:

1. Sara knows a decision is necessary. She's hesitant but knows that the sooner she makes a decision, the sooner she can get to work implementing it.

2. Jonathan continues to collect and analyze data because he's trying to find an option that will eliminate potential negative consequences.

3. Ingrid has a decision to make, but something always comes up that requires her attention. She's worried she'll never have time to make a decision.

4. Carla considers the issue and realizes that any required action is beyond her authority and brings it to the attention of the right person.

Answer:

Option 1: This option is correct. Although Sara is hesitant, she realizes that her best response is to make a decision.

Option 2: This option is incorrect. All decisions have consequences. Jonathan is procrastinating – perhaps he's either overwhelmed by the work involved or paralyzed by fear.

Option 3: This option is incorrect. Ingrid needs to prioritize the decision and stop putting it off. Procrastination will only make it worse.

Option 4: This option is correct. Carla has decided she isn't the person to make decisions about the matter. She's done the right thing in this circumstance.

Monitor progress

Once you've determined that a decision needs to be implemented and started the process by making the best choice, you can move on to the third action – implementing the decision. This involves monitoring progress and, if necessary, updating the implementation.

You should monitor the implementation of the decision. You can effectively monitor progress by developing an implementation plan and collecting real-time information.

The implementation plan helps monitor progress because it contains the information needed to determine when changes are necessary. In addition to key implementation milestones and critical review points, you should define what you need to monitor and how:

Establish how progress will be judged. It's important to establish a benchmark to objectively measure progress against.

Determine how frequently to monitor progress. Frequency depends on the magnitude of possible consequences or the level of uncertainty involved.

Establish who's responsible for reviewing and updating the information. This helps to eliminate any misunderstanding about where the responsibility lies.

Track resources invested versus benefits being realized. If investment is outweighing benefits, you should consider whether the decision is still viable.

Fiona needs to monitor the progress of a decision she's implementing. Fiona believes it will be important to remain flexible, so she just schedules when she thinks information should be collected.

Hector is also in the process of implementing a decision. He develops a detailed implementation plan to monitor progress. He establishes that success will be judged by noting the increases in production that occur without any increases in error. He'll collect and review information at predetermined milestones. He'll also track the resources required to produce a successful outcome. If resource use outweighs the benefit, he'll know something needs to change.

In these examples, Hector is much better prepared to monitor progress. Unlike Fiona, Hector has planned the implementation, established how success will be judged, and determined who will collect and review the information required. Hector has also decided to track resources so he can determine if the decision is proving to be beneficial. Fiona's failure to plan for implementation will make it difficult for her to judge success and take corrective action.

Decisiveness

Make sure the implementation is going as planned by collecting real-time information – data to help you remain informed about factors that can impact implementation. Even though this information is incomplete, it will help you monitor progress.

Your implementation plan defines the type of data to collect. For example, if you're implementing an investing decision, you'll want to collect real-time information about the investments involved. Focus on collecting data that will clearly show whether the decision is being implemented properly if things change. Because the plan defines a successful implementation, it's a great tool for monitoring progress.

Monitoring real-time data helps you discover problems or opportunities sooner. And the quicker you respond, the better.

Question

Stephanie has decided to make changes to an established procedure. It's intended to make production more efficient.

Which statements reflect appropriately implementing a decision?

Options:

1. Stephanie establishes guidelines for objectively monitoring progress

2. Stephanie defines how often to check progress, given the complexity of the solution

3. Stephanie makes sure responsibility is assigned to appropriate people

4. Stephanie provides a way to compare the resources being used to the benefits being gained

5. Stephanie includes best practices for implementing the decision

6. Stephanie designs a program to help her track key performance metrics as work is completed

Answer:

Option 1: This option is correct. The plan needs to establish how progress will be judged.

Option 2: This option is incorrect. The plan needs to outline how frequently progress should be monitored according to the severity of potential consequences.

Option 3: This option is correct. The implementation plan needs to define who's responsible for what.

Option 4: This option is correct. It's important to track resources and benefits to make sure the decision isn't more damaging than helpful.

Option 5: This option is incorrect. The implementation plan does not define how the work should be done, just how to monitor progress for success.

Option 6: This option is correct. It's important to monitor progress using real-time information when implementing a decision.

Updating the implementation

When monitoring progress, you may discover that a decision isn't working and needs to be changed or abandoned. However, individuals with a vested interest in the success of the decision may be resistant if they believe their egos or reputations will be damaged. And this can introduce bias. When bias exists, it's easy to make excuses to justify continuing. If this happens, consider using a neutral third party to review the facts and make an unbiased recommendation.

Consider this example. During the early stages of a decision to implement a new software solution, information indicates a design component is flawed. The designer in charge researches options for changing the design and determines the technology to overcome the issue isn't available. The decision is made to stop the project until the decision can be implemented as intended.

Now suppose a decision to cross-train workers is being implemented when reports of low retention rates, resistance to training, and elevated stress rates begin to mount. Because stakeholders are excited about the potential savings if this decision works, they refuse to give up on the project or make any changes.

In the first situation, the decision has the potential to be successful when the time is right. On the other hand, continuing with the implementation in spite of evidence that it isn't working – as in the second case – poses potential for limited success or even failure.

Why do decisions sometimes go wrong? Often, it's due to poor implementation. Sometimes it's a result of poor planning – not a poor choice. Instead of simply dismissing poor decisions, create value by learning from both personal experience and the experience of others.

Consider this example. Colleagues, Warren and Lita, work together as financial consultants. They've agreed to critique each other's decision making. Even though he's surprised by some of what Lita says, Warren carefully considers her suggestion that he study the decisions of others to broaden his approach. He also finds ways to use her input to improve his ability to make decisions.

However, Warren's evaluation of Lita's performance is received coldly. Lita accuses Warren of criticizing her unfairly. Warren has suggested she consider using a detailed implementation plan. Not seeing any value in what Warren has said, Lita dismisses it.

While Warren was proactive in seeking input and applying it, Lita has taken offense. Lita hasn't learned anything from her personal experience.

Learning what doesn't work from the experience of others is a great way to avoid the same mistakes. When significant trial and error goes into decisions, it's costly.

Decisiveness

Applying what you learn from the experience of others can help reduce wasted time, effort, and resources.

However, just because others have failed, it doesn't mean you will fail by making the same decision. When studying past decisions, carefully analyze why the decision was unsuccessful. Consider timing, implementation, who implemented it, and the time allowed to implement the decision. Each of these factors can have a significant influence on decisions.

Dylan is making a decision about what course of action can help to empower his employees. He researches popular approaches to empowering employees and finds that an overwhelming majority of them have failed. Deciding it's too risky, Dylan abandons the decision without going any further.

Joanna also needs to make a decision – how to engage in social media. Initially, her research shows that social media implementations often fail. However, Joanna critically assesses the reasons for failure and learns that factors such as tight deadlines and technical constraints played integral roles in these failures. Instead of abandoning the decision, Joanna analyzes her chance of success given her circumstances.

Dylan's choice to abandon implementation may be premature. It's possible he could have made the decision work. Joanna, on the other hand, has learned from the experience of others and has improved the likelihood that her decision will be successful.

Question

Which statements are examples of implementing a decision properly?

Options:

1. Ken realizes that using a premium material will put a construction project way over budget. He can't justify the cost, so he switches to a less expensive choice.

2. Helen is convinced her decision to improve sales by implementing an up-selling initiative will be successful, so she ignores real-time evidence to the contrary.

3. Joan has finally been asked to implement a recycling program. When she realizes that the cost will far outweigh the benefits, she pulls the plug.

4. Lola prefers not to consider how others have handled decisions because she finds it influences her too much.

5. Jerry always takes the time to review his decisions and applies what he learns to his decision-making process.

Answer:

Option 1: This option is correct. Because Ken is monitoring progress, he's able to recognize and address a problem before it negatively impacts the decision.

Option 2: This option is incorrect. Helen is being naive. Refusing to update implementation based on real-time information can lead to failure.

Option 3: This option is correct. Joan has made the right decision. Successfully monitoring progress involves knowing when to abandon the decision.

Option 4: This option is incorrect. Lola should try to be more critical when reviewing the decisions of others instead of using only what's relevant to her decisions.

Option 5: This option is correct. Learning from personal experience is a great way to improve your ability to make decisions.

CHAPTER TWO
Overcoming the Barriers to Decisiveness

Procrastination

Procrastination is a major barrier to decisiveness. Consider Laura, a graphic designer who was helping an electronics company redesign its logo in accordance with its rebranded image. When she had to decide which of her two mock-ups to propose, she kept putting off the decision. She would tell herself that she had to do more research about the company before she could decide, and that she wasn't ready. Gradually she recognized that she was procrastinating.

Putting off decisions is not conducive to decisiveness, and can become a habit that's hard to overcome. Among the reasons people procrastinate are the belief that there is plenty of time to make the decision and a fear of making a bad decision.

See each reason for procrastination to learn more about it.

Plenty of time

If you have an important decision to make but it doesn't need to be made immediately, you may be tempted by other tasks and activities. The sense is that you can do something later and not feel guilty about putting it off.

However, when you start delaying the decision, thinking that you have more than enough time, it can be difficult to get back on task when your deadline draws nearer. Instead of taking the time to make an informed decision, you can end up short on time and rushing through it. So if you think you can attend to some other things before the decision in question, make sure to set a specific time for attending to it.

Fear of making a bad decision

Fear of making a bad decision may have different causes. It likely stems from a lack of confidence that you have the ability or qualifications to make the decision.

This fear will prompt you to avoid making that decision for as long as possible. And if you left the decision until the last minute and it turns out to have been a bad one, you may even feel that you can blame it on being rushed. But waiting until the last minute is likely to impair your decision-making skills. You must fight the paralyzing fear of making a bad decision and give yourself enough time, especially when you have to make difficult decisions.

Question

People tend to procrastinate when they fear making a bad decision and are pressed for time.

Is this statement true or false?

Options:
1. True
2. False

Answer:

People tend to procrastinate when they're afraid of making a decision, but also when they feel they have plenty of time, not a shortage of it.

Self-discipline

One way of overcoming the tendency to procrastinate is to develop self-discipline. Cultivating self- discipline will help make you more decisive.

Self-discipline is about resisting the temptation to indulge in things that may provide some comfort or pleasure in the short term, but can ultimately have a negative impact.

Being self-disciplined can give you the ability to sacrifice immediate pleasures so that you achieve something even more satisfying in the future. For example, rather than leaving work a little early, you may use the time to get ahead on an important task.

In addition to helping you overcome procrastination and indecisiveness, learning self-discipline has several other important benefits. It helps you ignore distractions, finish what you start, and have greater confidence in your decisions.

Consider Naheed, a manager at a television news station. He's interviewing candidates for a new role at the station. Naheed learns that one candidate studied in the same program and under the same professor that he did. Though Naheed is tempted to use this familiarity as a shortcut to making his decision, he shows discipline by ignoring the distraction.

Instead he bases his decision on the merits of each candidate and takes the time to thoroughly review their portfolios. Choosing the best candidate takes time that Naheed might rather have spent another way. However, because he's self-disciplined, he's able to remain committed to finishing what he started.

Finally, Naheed's discipline to do what's needed gives him confidence in his decision. He knows he hasn't taken the easy way out, but rather has approached the decision in a thorough way. So he can confidently present his decision to the station's executives.

Question

What are the benefits of self-discipline for decision making?

Options:

1. You can stay focused on your task more easily
2. You'll be able to resist the lure of easy solutions
3. You understand that you need to stay focused on the task at hand
4. You'll be confident in your decisions
5. You'll make decisions more quickly
6. You can be certain that you'll make the right decisions

Answer:

Decisiveness

Option 1: This option is correct. Being disciplined can help you ignore distractions and stay on task so you can make the best possible decision.

Option 2: This option is correct. Self-discipline can help you resist easy but less effective solutions and do what's needed to make an informed decision.

Option 3: This option is correct. Self-discipline strengthens your commitment to your objective, which can help you stay on task until you achieve your goal.

Option 4: This option is correct. To be an effective decision maker, you must have confidence in your decisions. Self-discipline can give you this confidence because you know your decision-making process is rigorous.

Option 5: This option is incorrect. Self-discipline can help you overcome procrastination, and that can certainly speed up your decision making. But sometimes discipline can steer you away from the easy option and so require you to commit to a longer process.

Option 6: This option is incorrect. Self-discipline is a good way to become more decisive, and it should improve your decision making, but it doesn't necessarily mean that your decisions will always be the right ones.

Motivate yourself

While putting off decisions until a better or more comfortable time can be tempting, the different forms of procrastination are ultimately barriers to decisiveness. If you notice that you tend to procrastinate, there are three strategies you can use to overcome it: motivate yourself; recognize and eliminate excuses; and procrastinate later – that is, deliberately schedule time later for the activities that are tempting you to procrastinate now.

Learning to motivate yourself is an effective way to tackle procrastination. When you feel the urge to put something off, being able to remind yourself that what you're doing is important will help you resist the urge. Some people are more strongly motivated by the promise of rewards, while others need to be reminded of the consequences of their failure to achieve something.

See each type of motivation to learn more about it.

Rewards

If you're motivated by enjoying the benefits of your hard work, focus on these benefits as much as possible. These benefits might include the promise of a higher paycheck, a desired promotion, or the admiration of your coworkers. Or you may want to focus on more personal goals, such as a special vacation for you and your family if you secure a particular contract.

Whichever rewards you decide to focus on, aim to remind yourself of them when the desire to procrastinate arises. For example, post the salary of the position you're aiming for or a picture of the vacation destination you have in mind for your family next to your desk.

Consequences

Some people are strongly motivated by thinking about the consequences they might face if they fail to accomplish a task or make a decision. For example, ask yourself what will happen if you don't promptly decide which bidding company will receive a contract. Perhaps the project's schedule will be interrupted, or your boss will make the decision for you, making you look bad.

If you find that you're more easily motivated by consequences, try to focus on the ones that occur most immediately. More remote consequences – such as the danger of being passed over for a promotion in three months' time – are not such strong motivators. Instead, focus on more immediate consequences that will contribute to a larger, undesirable result.

Take Andrea for example. She's a regional manager for a chain of clothing retailers. After meeting with her superiors, she was told that she'd have to make some cuts to make up for a decline in sales. She needed to either let some employees go or make cuts to the store's available resources.

Andrea sat down and began listing reasons for and against these options. Making cuts to the store's resources would likely lead to further drops in sales, but it was equally hard to think of taking jobs away from her employees. Soon, Andrea found herself drifting off task and avoiding the difficult decision.

However, she reminded herself that if she didn't make a decision soon, sales would continue to fall and more people – including herself – could lose their jobs. By focusing on this immediate consequence, she was able to carefully consider her options and make a decision promptly.

Question

Al is a business trainer and has to decide what needs to be included in a new training program and what can be accomplished as part of continuous development.

Which thoughts could help keep him motivated to avoid procrastination?

Options:

1. Remind himself that if he doesn't stay on schedule with the program, he'll delay the entire department's priorities

2. Remind himself that if he develops the program on schedule, he'll be able to take a longer vacation

3. Remind himself that if he doesn't get the program ready on time, he may be jeopardizing his bonus next year

4. Remind himself that he can do the job properly and not to worry about failure

Answer:

Decisiveness

Option 1: This option is correct. Focusing on the consequences of failing to make his decision can help Al to stay mindful of what needs to be done.

Option 2: This option is correct. By reminding himself of the rewards of successfully making his decisions, Al can stay motivated to complete his task.

Option 3: This option is incorrect. While focusing on the potential consequences of his failure can help to keep Al motivated, it's important that these be relatively immediate consequences so that they're readily experienced if he falters.

Option 4: This option is incorrect. To stay motivated to overcome procrastination, Al should focus on either the consequences of not fulfilling his responsibilities or the rewards of succeeding.

Excuses

The second way to overcome procrastination is to recognize and eliminate excuses. Have you ever allowed your spouse request for you to pick up groceries on the way home or a colleague's request for help as excuses to avoid working on a decision? While it's easy to be tempted by these opportunities, most times it's up to you whether you give in to these temptations or rise above them.

When certain inconveniences arise, the tendency can be to see them as reasons to stop what you're doing and return to it later. If you're faced with an especially difficult decision, you may be likely to seek out or give in more easily than usual to such opportunities. So learning about excuses can help you recognize and get rid of them. Excuses tend to come from two general areas: other people and your environment.

See each source of excuses to learn more about it.

Other people

Decisiveness

People around you can provide you with excuses to avoid making an important decision. Perhaps a friend invites you to an afternoon baseball game, or a colleague asks if you can help with a task. Whether others come to you for help or to offer a distraction, you should ask yourself if you're simply looking for an excuse to get out of something before you agree.

If you notice yourself tending toward procrastination, try to lay out what needs to be done so that you can make an effective decision. If you can spare a bit of time, offer to help your colleague, or enjoy an afternoon outside. However, if you can't, try to be diligent and explain the situation.

Your environment

Certain things may occur that seem to be beyond your control. Traffic jams or problems with your computer are examples of this type of excuse. These can impede your progress. But by assessing them, you can decide whether they actually make your work impossible, or if they merely require a different approach.

For instance, say the Internet goes out in your office while you're researching a new supplier. Before giving up, ask yourself if there's another way you can get the information you need. Perhaps the company has hard copies of the data you need, or there is another task related to the decision that doesn't require the Internet. Then ask whether this approach will affect the quality of your work.

If a situation arises where you simply cannot continue with your task, move on to the next task on your priority list and plan to return to the delayed one later. If none of your tasks are possible, consider taking the afternoon or day off and making it up later in the week by staying late or coming in on a weekend.

Lewis is an editor in charge of the fiction list at a large publishing house. He needs to decide which books will be part of the company's fall catalog and which will be pushed for release in the new year. To do this, he needs to carefully consider a large selection of titles to determine which will appeal most to holiday shoppers.

When Lewis goes to conduct his review, he finds that many of the books he'd requested haven't arrived yet. Instead of putting off the task, however, he searches and finds that the company now makes digital copies of the manuscripts available to editors. By recognizing this as a possible excuse and asking whether there's another way to access the books, Lewis is able to stay on task.

Later that week, after many hours of careful reading, one of Lewis's editorial assistants comes to him with a problem. At first, Lewis welcomes this as an opportunity to delay his reading. However, after recognizing he's just looking for an excuse, he reminds himself of the urgency of his task. He refers his assistant to a colleague and completes his work.

Question

Lucinda works in the Marketing Department of a software development company. She urgently needs to decide on the best time to launch the company's new software package.

Which actions are examples of ways she can recognize and overcome excuses to procrastinate?

Options:

Decisiveness

1. She asks herself whether helping a colleague who comes to her for assistance is simply an opportunity for her to delay her decision
2. She asks to borrow a company laptop when her desktop computer crashes
3. She takes the afternoon off when the office's Internet service is interrupted
4. She helps her assistant determine the agenda of an upcoming meeting when he asks her for help

Answer:

Option 1: This option is correct. Other people can be blamed for causing delays. By asking whether she's looking for a reason to procrastinate, Lucinda can recognize and overcome this excuse.

Option 2: This option is correct. Lucinda avoids allowing a malfunction to become an excuse to delay her work. Instead, she finds an alternative way to stay on task.

Option 3: This option is incorrect. Lucinda should instead determine if there are other ways to accomplish her work, or consider if there's another task she could work on in the meantime.

Option 4: This option is incorrect. She should ask herself whether helping her assistant will contribute to making her decision and, since it won't, suggest he consult another person in the office.

Procrastinate later

Procrastination need not be strictly resisted at all times. In fact, allowing yourself to delay certain activities from time to time can help keep you motivated to complete your work and stay decisive. Sometimes, when you feel the urge to procrastinate, you can stay focused on your tasks, but allow yourself to procrastinate later.

If you find yourself facing a decision or working on a project that you think you'll want to delay, try this. First list how you'd procrastinate – for example, by organizing your desk or catching up on some filing. Then give yourself some time later to do one of these things. However, make a commitment to work for a fixed amount of time on your task beforehand.

Consider Lauren, an office administrator at a large sales company. She's been asked to find a new telephone and Internet contract for the office. To do so, she needs to contact a number of providers in the area and determine which can offer the company the best service at the best price.

When Lauren starts compiling a list of service providers to contact, she remembers that she has some phone calls to catch up on. But she realizes that this would be avoiding the work at hand.

However, she doesn't ignore the temptation. Instead, she decides she'll allow herself half an hour to deal with the phone calls after she has spent the next hour looking for companies to speak to. She also commits to returning to contacting service providers after the 30 minutes are up.

When you commit to spending a certain amount of time working before allowing yourself to move on to a procrastination-type task, ensure that it's a reasonable amount of time. Telling yourself that you'll work for four hours and only then allow yourself a diversion can result in an even greater urge to procrastinate. Short amounts of time spent working are effective and may give you the momentum needed to forgo the diversion altogether.

Question

Graham is a lead architect at a firm. The firm has been approached to design a new library for the city, and Graham needs to decide whether the firm has the resources to do the job.

What can Graham do to allow himself to procrastinate later to avoid delaying his decision?

Options:

1. Recognize that he'd likely be looking at examples of famous libraries, instead of concentrating on whether the firm can do the job

2. Commit to spending half an hour reviewing his and his employees' availability for the next year before allowing himself a diversion

3. Promise himself he'll put in five hours of work before allowing himself to move to one of his procrastination activities

4. Recognize his desire to procrastinate and refuse to submit to it, instead forcing himself to push ahead with his central task

Answer:

Option 1: This option is correct. By thinking about what he'd likely do to procrastinate, Graham can plan to allow himself this diversion later.

Option 2: This option is correct. By forcing himself to work for a short amount of time before some planned procrastination, Graham can accomplish something and generate momentum.

Option 3: This option is incorrect. While it's important to commit to working for a period of time before allowing a diversion, this should be a short amount of time that can be easily attained.

Option 4: This option is incorrect. It can be useful to allow some procrastination, as long as it comes after a period of productivity. Simply ignoring the urge can be ineffective because the temptation may grow stronger.

Obsessing about a decision

Have you ever been afraid of making the wrong decision? This fear can prevent you from thinking clearly and inhibit your judgment. While it's important to use care when making important decisions, you need to avoid becoming paralyzed by fear.

Being decisive involves accepting some risk. This means reconciling yourself with the fact that you may have to make undesirable decisions from time to time, or be able to accept certain outcomes. Doing so can help you let go of any fears you may have about making a decision. However, you first need to understand how fear can affect your decision making. Two manifestations of this fear are a tendency to obsess about decisions and a crippling fear of making bad decisions.

Obsessing about a decision causes your thoughts to become fixed on a single issue and is an obstacle to decisiveness.

Obsessive thinking is characterized by circular thinking. By continually returning to the starting point or initial question, obsessing can also provoke anxiety. This is because each potential course of action seems inappropriate or impossible, and so the circle starts again.

Counter the tendency to obsess by thinking clearly. Calmly and carefully evaluate a situation or set of options to reach a logical conclusion or plan of action.

Consider George, a manager with a construction company. George is responsible for sourcing construction materials for a large project. He recently discovered a lumber supplier that's 30% cheaper than the one he chose two months ago. He's trying to decide whether to cancel the current contract so he can purchase the rest of the lumber at the lower price. Consider the difference when he obsesses and when he thinks clearly about this decision.

See each type of thinking for an example of it.

Obsesses

At first, George is afraid his bosses will discover that he's paying too much for building materials. As such, he wants to cancel his current order and buy the rest of the lumber at a discount. However, doing so will result in long delays since he'll need to determine how much of the lumber has been used, how much can be returned, and how much more is required to finish the work. There may also be a charge for canceling the order.

On the other hand, if the new supplier isn't as reliable as the current one and George cancels the order, he may have to deal with an inferior product and service, which would raise costs even further. George worries each option will result in problems that could get him into trouble with his superiors.

Thinks clearly

Having considered the problem for a while, George decides to clearly set out his two options: stay with his current supplier, or choose the new, cheaper supplier. Next he compares the potential results of each choice. Staying with the current supplier would mean spending 30% more, but he wouldn't have to interrupt the building schedule or worry about returning unused materials. On the other hand, 30% off of the total cost represents a significant savings that would please his superiors.

George ultimately decides that these savings aren't worth the setback the project would likely face, nor can he be sure of the quality of the new supplier's product or service. By thinking clearly, George reaches a solution that he feels confident justifying to his superiors.

George's initial obsessing about the question is unproductive. He becomes stuck between thinking his bosses will be angry if he pays a higher price, and fearing that a switch in suppliers may create other problems.

By thinking clearly about his options and assessing them, George is able to make a decision that he feels is justified.

Clear thinking helps evade the anxiety that obsession and circular thinking can provoke.

Question

Ugo has been frustrated by the behavior of one of his colleagues lately. He's decided that something needs to be done, but he can't decide whether to approach the colleague directly or speak to his boss about it.

Which examples show Ugo obsessing about this decision?

Options:

1. He keeps coming back to the worries that if he tells his boss, she'll think he can't solve his own problems, but if he confronts his colleague, she'll lash out at him

2. He thinks it's impossible to make the right decision but grows more anxious each day that he doesn't make a decision

3. He decides to tell his boss because at least he can get some advice on how to broach the topic with his colleague

4. He reasons that he can simply tell his colleague that he's concerned about how they're working together, instead of accusing her of anything

Answer:

Option 1: This option is correct. Obsessing about decisions involves using circular thinking. Here, the focus never moves beyond the two rigid options.

Option 2: This option is correct. Obsessing about a decision often causes anxiety because progress is halted. In this case, Ugo can't make a decision and is made anxious by his inability to do so.

Option 3: This option is incorrect. Obsessing about a decision isn't productive. In this case, by thinking clearly, Ugo makes a decision and finds a positive aspect to it.

Option 4: This option is incorrect. Ugo demonstrates clear thinking rather than obsessing here, using reason to make an informed judgment about the available options.

Overcoming obsessive thinking

You can use three strategies to help you avoid obsessing about a decision. One is to deliberately distract yourself to take the pressure off. Another is to exercise or move around, which helps by expending some of the energy that fuels obsessive thinking. And third, it's a good idea to write down some steps or actions you'll take to help you reach a decision.

The first strategy you can use to avoid obsessive circular thinking is to consciously distract yourself.

To do this, try to choose something absorbing. This can be as simple as listening to some music, talking to a friend or colleague, or doing a simple task you've been putting off.

The task you use to divert your attention should be relatively simple and neutral. Because you know you still have an important decision to make, you may find it difficult to concentrate on a complex task.

Consider Leslie, for example. She owns and runs a small company that offers telecommunications solutions to companies. Recently her company has received more requests than it can fulfill. Leslie is trying to decide whether she should expand and hire more workers.

Leslie finds herself paralyzed by circular thinking. She wants to expand so she can take on the new clients. But this requires a big investment, and that's financially risky.

Finally she forces herself to stop going in circles. She shuts the door to her office and distracts herself by listening to her favorite opera. Before long, her mind is cleared from the decision.

Once Leslie has stopped her obsessive thinking, clear thinking can begin. And that's the kind of thinking that will help her make her decision.

Question

Andrew is trying to decide whether he should move his business to a new city and has begun to obsess about it.

True or false? To avoid obsessive thinking, Andrew should distract himself with another equally challenging task.

Options:

1. True
2. False

Answer:

Andrew should distract himself with a simple and neutral task, not another complex one.

Exercising and moving around is another strategy you can use to avoid obsessive thinking. Obsessing about a decision can cause anxiety and build up a lot of excess energy. By getting some exercise, you can expend some of this energy, which helps to calm you down. This can be as simple as going for a walk around the block, or stretching in your office.

Remember Leslie? Once she's taken her mind off her decision by listening to her favorite opera, she goes for a walk to a nearby park. By breathing in some fresh air and walking briskly, she feels herself calm down and her obsessive thoughts begin to fade away.

Question

Brenda is trying to decide whether she should fire an employee who has been regularly missing work.

What can she do to move from obsessing about this to thinking clearly?

Options:

1. Close her door and do her stretching routine
2. Walk to a café to get her lunch instead of eating in the office cafeteria
3. Plan to go for a run after deciding what to do about the employee
4. Make a plan for the next week that gives her time to exercise every day

Answer:

Option 1: This option is correct. A good way to think more clearly is to expend some energy.

Option 2: This option is correct. To think more clearly, Brenda needs to expend some energy. Going for a walk is a good way to do this.

Option 3: This option is incorrect. To keep from obsessing more about the decision, Brenda should stop and get some exercise rather than waiting until after she's made the decision.

Option 4: This option is incorrect. Brenda should get some exercise immediately to help with this decision rather than making a plan about the next week.

The third step for moving from obsessing to clear thinking is to write down some steps you'll take to help reach a decision.

This step can help you replace your obsessive thoughts with a set of concrete actions. Aim to come up with three or four things you will do. Make sure these are reasonable but not mundane steps that you can take.

If at first you're not sure what to do or where to begin, one of your steps could be to get more information about an aspect of your decision, or to speak with someone with experience in the matter.

When Leslie returns to her office after her walk, she makes a list of steps she can take to make her decision. She plans to begin by discussing the expansion with an acquaintance who enlarged his business last year.

Second, she plans to take a closer look at her accounts for the past three years to see if there has been a steady increase in business or whether the spike has been isolated to the past few months. Finally, Leslie plans to compare what she can expect to earn if she opens a new office with the costs of such an endeavor.

By making this list and completing each task, Leslie is able to think productively about her decision. This helps her reach a conclusion that she's confident about.

Question

Matthew owns a chain of restaurants and is trying to decide whether to renovate them so they all have similar décor.

Decisiveness

What can Matthew do to turn his obsessive thought process into clear thinking?
Options:
1. Talk to friends about how their favorite sports team is doing
2. List consulting decorators, construction companies, and suppliers as steps to help him make his decision
3. Just make the decision before moving on to any other considerations
4. Focus his attention on whether to do it or not since this is the basis of the decision 5. Go for a walk around one of his restaurants

Answer:

Option 1: This option is correct. A good way to move toward clearer thinking is to distract yourself from the decision with something simple and neutral.

Option 2: This option is correct. Jotting down steps to help make a decision is an example of moving beyond obsessing to clear thinking.

Option 3: This option is incorrect. When obsessing about a decision, it's helpful to list the things you can do to make it, rather than forcing a decision.

Option 4: This option is incorrect. Since he's obsessing about the decision, Matthew should try to get away from the circular thinking between the two options, rather than limiting himself to them.

Option 5: This option is correct. Getting some exercise and moving around is a good strategy for avoiding obsessing about a decision since it uses up energy that might result in circular thought.

Fear making a bad decision

Being afraid of making a bad decision is the second way that fear manifests itself in decision making. For example, Ethel is trying to decide whether to apply for a new job. She doesn't see much room for advancement in her current position and wants to move forward with her career. However, she's worried that she could wind up worse off than she is now.

To overcome the fear of making a bad decision, it's important to realize that there aren't good or bad decisions. Rather, it's what comes as a result of your decisions that's good or bad.

The outcomes of particular decisions are often beyond your control. They may depend on the decisions and actions of others.

All you can do is make the best decisions you can based on the information you have. This is what you control.

Decisiveness

Decisions that seem good can end up having bad outcomes, just as decisions that seem bad can turn out to have great outcomes.

See each kind of decision for examples of how outcomes can be surprising.

Decisions that seem good

Eduardo has developed a device that can be used to charge a variety of electronic items. A number of distributors make offers to carry it in their stores. But then a large, international retailer makes a lucrative offer for exclusive rights to the device, which Eduardo eventually settles on.

However, three months later, Eduardo is frustrated because his product is still not on the market. Meanwhile, a number of rival products have surfaced and threaten to render his obsolete.

Decisions that seem bad

Josephine is a hiring manager with an event management company and is in charge of hiring two new event coordinators. However, a slow response to the job postings yields a disappointing field of candidates. She is faced with the decision of reposting the positions, putting the company behind schedule, or hiring candidates who may not be right for the job.

Josephine ultimately hires two of the candidates. She's pleasantly surprised with the enthusiasm they bring to their roles and their willingness to learn by shadowing other event coordinators. These two turn out to be two of the strongest coordinators that the company has.

When you understand that you can control the decisions you make but not the ultimate results of these decisions, you can free yourself from the fear of making a bad decision.

Of course, acknowledging that you cannot control the outcome doesn't guarantee that things will turn out as you'd like them to. But it can help you avoid worrying all the time.

Learning to focus on what you can control doesn't mean that you should be complacent regarding the results of your decisions. Instead, you can accept that sometimes you won't get what you want. You should do what you think is right, and accept the results.

To overcome the fear of making a bad decision, try to pay attention to your thoughts. First, identify a decision that you fear making. Then reframe your thinking so that your focus is on what you can do, rather than on the outcome. It can take some practice to shift your focus toward what's actually under your control, but this is a powerful way to become more decisive.

For instance, if you think "I just don't know what to do," try to shift your thinking. You can replace it with, "I'll do everything I can to make the best decision I'm able to."

Or if you think "I'm just not the right person to make this decision," you might be tempted to think you should ask your boss to do it, or at least ask her to advise you.

However, if you work to reconsider your thinking, an effective statement might be, "I'm being trusted to make this decision and I have the right tools to do it."

For example, Peter runs an online entertainment magazine and has recently been encouraged to include a section on video games. While this falls outside his area of expertise, it seems he could increase his audience by doing it.

Decisiveness

At first Peter thinks, "If I make this change, I really need my readership to pick up to cover the costs." However, he quickly notices that this statement focuses only on the outcome of his decision.

Instead, Peter reframes his thought. He thinks, "I'm going to do some research to see if I can appeal to a new demographic by making this change and if it seems like a good idea, I'll do it." By focusing on what he can do, Peter effectively dispels his fear about the decision.

Question

Catherine runs a small business that sells homemade beauty products. Recently she's been told that she should create a web site so she can sell her products online. She's anxious, however, because this could affect the image of her products, which are traditional and simple, and alienate clients who value this.

How could Catherine reframe her thinking to overcome her fear of making a bad decision?

Options:

1. "I'll do my best to create a web site that's as true as possible to the qualities that define my products."

2. "I'm not too worried about how this turns out since it's not my area of expertise."

3. "I know that setting up a good web site won't alienate my best customers since the products will be the same."

Answer:

Option 1: This is the correct option. In this statement, Catherine focuses on what she can do and not on possible outcomes of the decision.

Option 2: This option is incorrect. Letting go of the outcome isn't the same as becoming indifferent to the decision, as Catherine is here.

Option 3: This option is incorrect. This statement reflects that Catherine is still focused on the outcome of her decision rather than on what she can do.

Information overload

You might think that the more information you have, the better prepared you are to make a decision. However, too much information can actually lead to confusion and uncertainty. This is called information overload. Being overwhelmed by information is a barrier to decisiveness.

There is no "right" amount of information to have. It varies according to the person and the decision to be made. However, each person has a point at which information received exceeds the capacity to absorb it. Signs of information overload include experiencing confusion despite an abundance of information. The Inability to relax after you've finished work and difficulty sleeping are two other signs.

Se each sign of information overload to learn more about it.

Confusion

If you have a lot of information but still feel confused, you may be overloaded.

For example, Stefan works for a property management company. He's trying to decide whether the company should purchase an apartment building. To determine if the property is profitable, Stefan looks at others in the neighborhood to find out about their valuation and taxes. He also speaks to a range of specialists to assess the state of the building.

Despite the mass of information he accumulates, Stefan feels more confused than ever about what he should do.

Inability to relax

Information overload can make you unable to relax, even after you've finished your work. You find yourself continuing to trawl through the information in your head.

For example, Helga works for a company that sells stylish home design products. Helga's boss asks her to find a local manufacturer to produce a newly designed product. Helga starts by calling manufacturers to get quotes on how long it would take them to fill an order, and what it would cost. She also tries to get a sense of people's opinions of each manufacturer. Then she compares their rates with those of manufacturers located further away.

Helga speaks with more than 30 manufacturers and has a list of more to contact. Having so much to keep track of begins to wear on her. Eventually her boss asks if she's OK since her colleagues begin to sense her tension.

Difficulty sleeping

Finding it hard to sleep at night because you're still thinking about the information involved in your decision is another sign that you may be overloaded.

For instance, Anthony is an investment banker helping a client diversify her portfolio. She wants to invest in reliable and slow-building companies. Being relatively new to the role, Anthony decides to supplement his training with some in-depth research about one company in particular. He consults business reviews, earnings reports, and growth forecasts. He even speaks to some former employees of the company to get a better sense of their stability.

Finally, he gives his client a list of potential investment opportunities. However, in subsequent nights, he doesn't sleep well. He continues to think about different reports and projections he consulted and begins to second-guess his suggestions.

Question

Roberto works in a midsize office and has been asked to assess its computers and network status. His task is to determine whether the company needs to replace its existing computers and network hardware, or if it can get by with updating the software.

Which statements suggest that Roberto is suffering from information overload?

Options:

1. While he has consulted industry reports, consumer reports, and every major retailer, Roberto feels like he can't make a confident decision

2. Even after Roberto makes the decision, he remains tense for several days

3. He continues to wake up at night thinking he forgot to consider a particular retailer's offer

4. Only after reading the consumer reports does Roberto finally feel confident that he can decide accurately

5. Despite consulting a wealth of resources on the matter, Roberto makes the wrong decision
Answer:
Option 1: This option is correct. A sign of information overload is remaining confused despite having lots of information. In this case, Roberto is still unsure of what to do in spite of his extensive research.

Option 2: This option is correct. A sign of information overload is being unable to relax, even after you've finished your work. Here, Roberto's continued tension indicates this.

Option 3: This option is correct. Being unable to sleep well is a sign of information overload. Roberto's anxiety about not checking one thing suggests he's overloaded.

Option 4: This option is incorrect. Information overload tends to lead to uncertainty, tension, and sleeplessness. In this case, Roberto's confidence suggests he's not suffering from information overload.

Option 5: This option is incorrect. Information overload doesn't necessarily correlate with making misguided decisions. It can result in tension and sleeplessness, but the quality of decisions isn't necessarily impacted.

Avoiding information overload

You can take four steps to avoid information overload while making decisions. First, list the reasons that you're taking too long to make a particular decision. Second, write a sentence to contradict each reason. Third, set a deadline for making the decision. And fourth, budget time for each decision-making task within the deadline.

Consider a case where you have a decision to make but where you're overwhelmed by all the information you have on the issue. The first step is to list the reasons why you're taking too long to make this decision. Perhaps you're being a perfectionist about the decision. Or maybe you've become paralyzed by continually asking yourself "What if?" Alternatively, you may be avoiding some other task.

Having identified the reasons for taking too long to make a decision, the second step is to consider each reason and write a statement to contradict it. For some statements, this might be a matter of simply writing down its opposite. For example, if you said, "I'm going to make the wrong decision," you might replace it with "I'm not going to make the wrong decision."

Other times you may need to be more inventive. Perhaps you said "I'm just not prepared or qualified to make this decision." Instead say, "I've compiled sufficient information on the matter to make an informed and capable decision."

The purpose of this step is to recognize how your negative thoughts can be transformed into realistic statements. If you recognize that your thinking is keeping you from being decisive, you can take action to correct it.

For example, Yvette is starting a language training company. She's trying to determine what languages to offer, and in what format. In her ongoing research, however, she's found that what people want to study and why is more complicated than she expected. After more than a month of research, Yvette realizes she's become overwhelmed by information. To move forward, she lists her reasons for taking so long, and then contradicts them with written statements.

See each of Yvette's steps to learn more about how to identify and replace reasons for taking too long with decisions.

List reasons for taking too long

Yvette spends a lot of time reading journals on the issue, consulting other schools, and speaking to friends and family. She even posts online surveys to ask students what and why they started studying. Currently, Yvette is surrounded by so much information that she's filled with more uncertainty than when she began.

Decisiveness

She realizes that she thinks everything has to be perfect if her new business venture is to succeed. And while she wants to make the right decision about what to offer, she realizes that her anxiety about making the wrong decision is preventing her from making any decision. Yvette is afraid that by choosing one option she would be excluding a potentially lucrative option or segment of customers.

Contradict them

Yvette replaces the statement "Everything has to be perfect for my new business to succeed" with, "Everything doesn't have to be perfect for this to succeed." She also adds that "It's impossible for everything to be perfect, and business success depends on many other things."

More simply, Yvette replaces the statement "I'm going to make the wrong decision" with, "I'm not going to make the wrong decision." Finally, Yvette considers that she's afraid of losing some customer groups by making a choice. She contradicts this by telling herself that she won't be losing customers, but rather gaining ones by tailoring courses to their needs. What's more, she's only losing customers by failing to make this decision.

Question

Lester is a research director for an electronics company. He's trying to decide whether his company should begin to invest more time in a burgeoning technology.

Which actions correspond to the first two steps of avoiding information overload while making decisions?

Options:

1. He realizes that what's holding him up is that he doesn't feel qualified to make this decision

2. He tells himself that he can make this decision because of his skills and experience

3. He identifies areas in which he needs to learn more so that he can become better able to make the decision

4. He tells his boss that he doesn't feel like he's the right person to be making this decision

Answer:

Option 1: This option is correct. The first step to avoiding information overload is identifying the reasons why you're taking so long to do it. In this case, Lester is worried about his ability to make the decision.

Option 2: This option is correct. The second step for overcoming information overload is to contradict the reasons listed – in this case, that Lester is not qualified to make the decision.

Option 3: This option is incorrect. Conducting more research isn't one of the steps to avoiding information overload.

Option 4: This option is incorrect. The first two steps for overcoming information overload are to identify and then contradict reasons that are holding you back. When you try to back out of making the decision, you succumb to negative thinking rather than countering it.

Budgeting your time

Once you've identified and contradicted the reasons for taking too long to make a decision, the third step is to set a deadline for the decision. Make sure to allow yourself a reasonable amount of time – but don't allow too much, as that will encourage procrastination. Once you've set out how long you're going to allow yourself to reach a decision, the fourth step is to budget time for each decision-making task within your deadline.

There are essentially four decision-making tasks: define your objective, create your options, assess your options, and finally, choose the best option. By setting up a time line for each of these steps, you'll find it easier to resist the temptation to keep looking for more information and instead focus on what you've already got.

Recall Yvette, who's starting a language school. She has completed the first two steps to avoid information overload, listing the reasons for delay and contradicting them. She now performs the third step by recognizing that she has only three days to complete the process if she's to advertise courses in time. Finally, she completes the fourth step by allowing herself the rest of the day to create her options, the next day to assess the options, and Friday to choose the best option.

Now consider this example. William is a travel agent. He wants to introduce a new tour to his customers, but can't decide which tour to choose. William decides to take action to try to avoid information overload.

He starts by recognizing that he's struggling with the decision because he thinks it could make or break his business. He quickly counters this mindset, however. To do this, he tells himself that it's unlikely that this one decision could ruin his company. He decides he needs to focus instead on making the best decision he can.

Next, he decides he needs to make a decision within three weeks. So William plans to take two weeks to investigate the potential vacation packages he can offer. Then he'll allow himself a week to assess these and choose one.

However, William runs out of time before making a satisfactory decision. This is because while he starts out right by creating his options, he fails to set aside specific time for choosing an option, instead bundling this task together with his assessment of the options. As a result, he scrambles at the last minute and the decision suffers.

Question

Ingrid is a process improvement specialist. She's helping to develop a customer survey for a client and needs to decide on the best method for this particular survey. But she's been struggling to move beyond her review of what she did in similar past instances.

Which actions relate to the third and fourth steps of overcoming information overload?

Options:

1. She allows herself two days to make up her mind
2. She gives herself four hours to generate options, one day to assess them, and an afternoon to choose the best one
3. She informs her client that she needs more time in order to properly research options for his needs
4. She consults outside help for an opinion on the things that she's examined so far and to solicit advice on what else to consider

Answer:

Option 1: This option is correct. Setting a deadline for the decision is the third step.

Option 2: This option is correct. Budgeting time for each decision-making task within the deadline is the

fourth step for overcoming information overload.

Option 3: This option is incorrect. The third and fourth steps are about setting yourself a deadline and budgeting your time to accomplish your tasks within that schedule. Asking for more time isn't part of this.

Option 4: This option is incorrect. The third and fourth steps are about setting a deadline and budgeting your time to make a decision. Consulting outside help to access more information isn't part of these steps.